CDL Book Club
Presents
The CDL Exam Book

Jeff Mills

Published by Starry Night Publishing.Com

Rochester: New York

Copyright 2020 – Jeff Mills

This book remains the copyrighted property of the author, and may not be reproduced, copied and distributed for commercial, or noncommercial purposes. Thank you for your support.

Jeff Mills

The CDL Exam Book

Contents

Frequently Asked Questions ………………………………………………………………….. 5

General Knowledge …………………………………………………………………………… 7

Air Brake Test …………………………..………………………………………………….… 29

Combination Test …………………………………………………………………………… 35

Jeff Mills

Commercial Vehicle *Training Program*

FREQUENTLY ASKED QUESTIONS

What number do I call for more information, registration and billing, orientation or intake interviews?
240-581-2452

What endorsements should I test for when obtaining my CDL Learner's Permit?
You should be tested on the following knowledge test/endorsements:
CDL-A: General Knowledge, Air Breaks, Combinations (Mandatory)
Tanker, Doubles and Triples, and Hazmat (Optional)
CDL-B Hospitality: General Knowledge, Air Breaks, Passenger (Mandatory)
***You must obtain an 80% passing score on each required test.

Note: **CDL-A or B** *training does provide training for an S (School Bus) endorsement.*
CDL B Hospitality/Tourism Training *primarily uses a CDL Bus with an automatic transmission. Time permitting students may train on a CDL Heavy Straight Truck with manual transmission.*

Does CDL Book Club, have a course I can take to help me prepare to take the MVA's CDL Learner's Permit test?
Yes, our CDL Learner's Permit preparation course is held over 4 week sessions. It provides instruction in to help you to take the LP test and the written tests for any required endorsements.
After you have passed the MVA written test and obtained your CDL Learner's Permit with the appropriate endorsements, you are eligible to enroll in Behind the Wheel Commercial Vehicle Training Program. Remember, you must have a current DOT Physical Card when you go to the MVA to take the LP test.

Where to get your Physicals done at?
Concentra or Patients First

If you do not finish the program will there be a refund?
If a student does not complete the CDL program, no monies will be refunded.

Jeff Mills

The CDL Exam Book

General Knowledge

1. You are driving on a straight, level highway at 50 mph. There are no vehicles in front of you suddenly a tire blew out on your vehicle. What should you do first?
    a. **Stay off the brake until the vehicle has slowed down.**
    b. Begin light braking.
    c. Begin emergency braking.

2. You are driving a new truck with a manual transmission. What gear you probably have to use to take a long steep downhill grade?
    a. The same gear you would use to climb the hill.
    b. **A lower gear than you would use to climb the hill.**
    c. A higher gear than you would use to climb the hill.

3. You are checking your wheels and rims for a pre-trip inspection. Which of these statements is true?
    a. **Rust around wheel nuts may mean that they are loose.**
    b. A vehicle can be safely driven with one missing lug nut on a wheel.
    c. Mismatched lock rings can be used on the same vehicle.

4. You are checking your tires for a pre-trip inspection. Which of these statements is true?
    a. **Tires of mismatched sizes should not be used together in the same vehicle.**
    b. Radial and bias-ply tires can be used together on the same vehicle.
    c. 2/32 inch tread depth is safe for front tires.

5. If a straight vehicle (not trailer or articulation) goes into front-wheel skid, it will:
    a. Slide sideways and spin out.
    b. **Go straight ahead even if the steering wheel is turned.**
    c. Go straight ahead but will turn if you turn the steering wheel.

6. If you need to leave the road in the traffic emergency, you should:
    a. Try to get all wheels off the pavement.
    b. **Avoid braking until you speed has dropped to about 20 mph.**
    c. Avoid a shoulder because most shoulders will not support a large vehicle.

7. Which of these statements about certain types of cargo is true?
    a. **Unstable load such as hanging meat or livestock can require extra caution on curves.**
    b. Oversize load con be hauled without special permit during time when the roads are not busy.
    c. When liquids are hauled, the tank should always be loaded totally full.

8. According to the driver's manual, why you should limit the use of your horn?
    a. **It can startle other drivers.**
    b. The horn is not a good way to let others know you are there.
    c. You should keep firm grip on the steering wheel with both hand at all times.

9. You do not have a hazardous materials endorsement on your commercial driver's license. You are asked to deliver hazardous materials in a placarded vehicle. You should:
    a. **Refuse to haul the load.**
    b. Haul the load but only to the nearest place where a driver with hazardous material endorsement can take over.
    c. Haul the load but file a report with the department of transportation after the trip.

10. Which of these statements about staying alert to drive is true?
    a. A half-hour break for coffee will do more to keep you alert than a half-hour nap.
    b. **If you must stop to take a nap, it should be at a truck stop or other rest area and never on the side of the road.**
    c. Steep is the only thing that can overcome fatigue.

11. Your vehicle has hydraulic brakes. While traveling on a level road, you press the brake pedal and find that it goes to the floor. Which of these statement is true?
    a. **Pumping the brake pedal may bring the pressure up so you can stop the vehicle.**
    b. The parking brake will not work nor either because it is part of the same hydraulic system.
    c. Shifting into neutral will help to slow the vehicle.

12. You are driving a vehicle at 55 mph on pavement. About how much total stopping distance will you need to bring it to a stop?
    a. Twice the length of the vehicle.
    b. Half the length of the football field.
    c. The length of a football field.

13. Which of these statements about cold weather driving is true?
    a. An engine cannot overheat when the weather is very cold.
    b. Windshield washer antifreeze should be used.
    c. Exhaust system leaks are less dangerous in cold weather.

14. When driving at night, you should:
    a. Look to the left side of the road when a vehicle is coming toward you.
    b. Adjust your speed to keep your stopping distance within your sight distance.
    c. Deem your lights within 300 feet of oncoming vehicle.

15. Which of these statement about downshifting is true?
    a. When you downshift for a curve, you should do so before you enter the curve.
    b. When you downshift for a hill, you should do so after you start down the hill.
    c. When double-clutching, you should let the ramps decrease while the clutch is released and the shift level is in neutral.

16. For your safety, when setting out reflective triangles you should:
    a. Hold the triangles between yourself and oncoming traffic.
    b. Keep them out of sight while you walk to the spots where you are going to set them.
    c. Turn on your flashers.

17. As the blood alcohol concentration (SAC) goes up, what happens?
    a. The drinker more clearly sees how alcohol is affecting him/her.
    b. The effects of alcohol decrease.
    c. Judgment and-self control are affected.

18. Which of these is good thing to remember about using mirrors?
    a. you should look at mirror for several seconds at a time.
    b. Convex mirror make things look larger and closer than they really are.
    c. There are blind spots that your mirror cannot show.

19. Hydroplaning:
    a. Only occurs when there is a lot of water.
    b. Cannot occur when driving through a puddle.
    c. Is more likely if tires pressure is low.

20. if you are being tailgated, you should:
    a. Increase your following distance.
    b. Flash your brake lights.
    c. Signal the tailgater when is safe to pass you.

21. A key principle to remember about loading cargo is to keep the load.
    a. To the front
    b. To the rear
    c. Balance in the cargo area.

22. How far should a driver look ahead of the vehicle while driving?
    a. 5-8 seconds.
    b. 12-15 seconds.
    c. 18-21 seconds.

23. How do you correct a rear-wheel acceleration skid?
 a. Apply more power to the wheels.
 b. Stop accelerating.
 c. Downshift.

24. The Purpose of the retarders is to:
 a. Help slow the vehicle while driving and reduce brake wear.
 b. Apply extra braking power to non-drive axles.
 c. Help prevent skids.

25. Controlled braking:
 a. Can be used when you are turning sharply.
 b. Involves locking the wheels for short period of time.
 c. Is used to keep a vehicle in a straight line when braking.

26. Which of these is good thing to do when steering to avoid a crash?
 a. Apply the brakes while turning.
 b. Steer with one hand so that you can turn the wheel more quickly.
 c. Don't turn anymore than needed to clear what is in your way.

27. You should stop driving:
 a. After 5 hours.
 b. After 9 hours.
 c. Whenever you become sleepy.

28. Which of these is NOT a good rule to follow when caring for injured person at an accident scene?
 a. If a qualified person is helping them, stay out of the way unless asked to assist.
 b. Keep an injured person cool.
 c. Move severely injured person if there is a danger due to fire or passing traffic.

29. You should avoid driving through deep puddles or flowing water. But if you must, which of these steps can help to keep your brakes working?
 a. Gently putting on the brakes while driving though the water.
 b. Applying hard pressure on both the brake pedal and acceleration after coming of water.
 c. Turning on your brake heater.

30. Which of these statements about drugs is true?
 a. A driver can use any prescription drug while driving.
 b. Amphetamine, ("pep pills" or "beanies") can be used to help driver stay alert.
 c. Use of drug can lead to an accident and/or arrest.

31. Which of these is good thing to remember when crossing or entering traffic with a heavy vehicle?
 a. Heavy vehicle need larger gaps in traffic than cars.
 b. The best way to cross the traffic is to pull the vehicle partway across the road and block one lane while waiting for the other to clear.
 c. Because heavy vehicles are easy to see, you can count on other drivers to move out of your way or slow down for you.

32. You are driving a heavy vehicle with a manual transmission. You have to stop the vehicle on the shoulder while driving on an uphill grade. Which of these is a good rule to follow when putting it back in motion up the grade?
 a. Keep the clutch slipping while slowly accelerating.
 b. Use the parking brake to hold the vehicle until the clutch engages.
 c. Let the vehicle go backwards a few feet before you engage the clutch, but turn the wheel so that the back moves away from the roadway.

Jeff Mills

33. You are driving a heavy vehicle. You must exit a highway using a off-ramp that curves downhill. You should:
   a. **Slow down to a safe speed before the curve.**
   b. Slow to the posted speed limit for the off-ramp.
   c. Wait until you are in the curve before downshifting.

34. You must park on a side of a level, straight four-lane divided highway. Where should you place the reflective triangles?
   a. **One within 10 feet of the rear of the vehicle, one about 100 feet to the rear, and one about 200 feet to the rear.**
   b. One within of 10 feet of the rear of the vehicle, one about 100 feet to the rear, and one about 100 feet to the front of the vehicle.
   c. One about 10 feet of the front of the vehicle, one about 100 feet to the rear, and one about 200 feet to the rear.

35. You are driving on a two-lane road. An oncoming driver drifts into your lane and is headed straight for you. Which of these is most often the best option to take?
   a. Hard braking.
   b. **Steer to the right.**
   c. Steer onto the left shoulder.

36. Brake "fade"
   a. **Can be caused by the brakes getting very hot.**
   b. Can be correcting by letting upon the brakes for 1-2 seconds and then replying them.
   c. Is a problem that only occurs with drum brakes

37. Which of these statement about engine overheating is true?
   a. You should never shut off an overheated engine until it cools.
   b. **You should never remove the radiator cap on a pressure system until the system is cooled.**
   c. Antifreeze is not needed when the weather is warm.

38. Which of these statements about overhead clearance is true?
   a. You should assume posted clearance sign are correct.
   b. **The weight of a vehicle changes its height.**
   c. If the road surface causes your vehicle to tilt toward objects at the edge of the road, you should drive close to shoulder

39. Which of these statement about vehicle fire is true?
   a. If cargo in a van or a box trailer catches on fire, you should open the cargo door as soon as possible.
   b. If your engine is on fire, you should open the hood as soon as you can.
   c. **A burning tire should be cooled with water.**

40. You are driving a long vehicle that makes wide turns. You want to make left from Elm Street onto Poplar Street. Both are two-lane two ?way streets. You should:
   a. Begin turning your vehicle as soon as your enter the intersection.
   b. **Begin turning your vehicle when you are halfway through the intersection.**
   c. Turn into the left lane of Poplar Street and then move to the right lane when the traffic is clear.

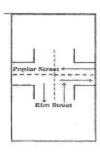

41. You must drive on a slippery road. Which of these is a good thing to do in such a situation?
   a. Use a smaller follow distance.
   b. Apply the brakes while on curves.
   c. **Slow down gradually.**

42. Which of these statements about acceleration is true?
   a. When traction is poor, more power should be applied to the accelerator.
   b. **Rough acceleration can cause mechanical damage.**
   c. You should feel a jerking motion if you accelerate your vehicle properly.

54. To avoid a crash, you had to drive into the right shoulder. You are now driving at 40 mph on the shoulder. How should you move back into the pavement?
    a. If the shoulder is clear, stay on the right until your vehicle comes to a stop then move back into the pavement when it is safe.
    b. Brake hard to slow the vehicle, then steer sharply onto the pavement.
    c. Steer sharply onto the pavement, then brake hard as you Countersteer.

55. Which of these statements about driving in areas with strong wind is true?
    a. You should drive alongside other vehicles to help break up the wind.
    b. The lighter you vehicle, the less trouble you will have with the wind.
    c. Wind are specially a problem when coming out tunnels.

56. which of these is a good thing to do when driving at night?
    a. Keep your speed slow enough that you can stop within the range of your headlights.
    b. Look directly at the oncoming headlights only briefly.
    c. Keep instrument lights bright.

57. You are driving a 40-foot vehicle at 35 mph. The road is dry and visibility is good What is the least amount of space you should keep in front of your vehicle to be safe?
    a. 3 seconds.
    b. 4 seconds.
    c. 5 seconds.

58. What is the proper way to hold a steering wheel?
    a. With both hands close together, near the top of the wheel.
    b. With both hands close together, near the bottom of the wheel.
    c. With both hands on opposite sides of the wheel.

59. High beams should be:
    a. Used when it is safe and legal to do so.
    b. Turned on when an oncoming driver does not dim his/her lights.
    c. Dimmed at the time when you get within 100 feet of another vehicle.

60. You can see a marking on vehicle ahead of you. The marking is a red triangle with an orange center. What does the marking mean?
    a. It may be a slow moving vehicle.
    b. The vehicle is hauling hazardous materials.
    c. It is being driven by a student driver.

61. Which of these is NOT part of the pre-trip inspection of the engine compartment?
    a. Valve clearance.
    b. Engine oil level.
    c. Worn electrical wiring insulation.

62. The road you are driving on becomes very slippery due to glare ice. Which of these is a good thing to do in such a situation?
    a. Stop driving as soon as you can safety do so.
    b. Downshift to stop.
    c. Keep varying you speed by accelerating and braking.

63. You wish to turn right, from one two-lane, two-way street to another. You vehicle is so long that you must swing wide to make the turn. Which of these figures shows how the turn should be made.
    a. Figure A.
    b. Figure B.
    c. Figure C.

64. You are driving a vehicle that could safely be driving at 55 mph on an open road. But traffic is heavy and other vehicles drivers at the speed 35 mph, though the speed limit is 55mph. The safes speed for your vehicle is more likely to be:
    a. 35 mph.
    b. 45 mph.
    c. 55 mph.

65. What is countersteering?
    a. Turning the steering wheel counterclockwise.
    b. Using the steering axle brakes to prevent oversteering.
    c. Turning the wheel back in the other direction after steering to avoid a traffic emergency.

66. Which of these statements about backing a heavy vehicle is true?
    a. You should avoid backing whenever you can.
    b. Helpers should be out of the driver's sight and use only voice (spoken) signals to communicate with the driver.
    c. It is safer to back toward the right side of the vehicle than toward the driver's side.

67. Which of these statements about marking a stopped vehicle is true?
    a. If a hill or curve keeps drivers behind you from seeing the vehicle within 500 feet, the rear reflective triangle should be moved down the road to give adequate warning.
    b. You do not need to put out reflective triangles unless the vehicle will be stopped for 30 minutes or more.
    c. The vehicle's taillights should be kept on to warn other drivers.

68. Which of these best describes how you should use the brake pedal on a steep downhill grade?
    a. Light, pumping action.
    b. Light, steady pressure.
    c. Repeated strong pressure then release.

69. Which of these statements about using turn signals is true?
    a. You do not need to use your turn signal early.
    b. When turning, you should signal early.
    c. You should use your turn signal to mark your vehicle when it is pulled off on the side of the road.

70. Which of these statements about double clutching and shifting is true?
    a. You can use the tachometer to tell you when to shift.
    b. Double clutching should not be use when the road is slippery.
    c. Double clutching should only be used with a heavy load.

71. Which of these statements about speed management is true?
    a. Empty trucks always stop in a shorter distance than fully loaded.
    b. When you double your speed (go twice as fast), it will take twice the distance to stop.
    c. You should choose a speed that lets you stop within the distance that you can see ahead.

72. Retarders:
    a. Can cause the driver wheels to skid when they have poor traction.
    b. Cause extra brake wear.
    c. Work when you apply the brake pedal.

73. To correct a drive wheel braking skid, you should:
    a. Stop braking, turn quickly, then Countersteer.
    b. Increase braking.
    c. Increase braking, turn quickly, and Countersteer.

74. When exiting or entering on a curved freeway ramp, you should:
    a. Maintain a speed 5-10 mph under the posted speed limit.
    b. Maintain the posted speed limit.
    c. Slow down at least 50% of the posted speed limit.

75. Which of the following vehicles will have the longer stopping distance?
    a. Empty truck.
    b. Loaded truck.
    c. Bobtail

76. How many red reflective triangles are you required to carry?
    a. 2
    b. 3
    c. 4.

77. You are required to inspect your truck within how many miles after beginning the trip?
    a. 100
    b. 150
    c. 25

78. There are two types of jackknife; they are:
    a. Trailer.
    b. Tractor.
    c. Both A and B.

79. The new BAC (Blood Alcohol Concentration) for commercial drivers to be considered intoxicated when driving a commercial vehicle is:
    a. 0.04
    b. 0.01
    c. 0.10

80. Where should the ignition key be during the pre-trip inspection?
    a. In your pocket.
    b. In the ignition.
    c. On the driver's seat.

81. When loading a trailer, if the cargo is loaded all the rear, it may result in:
    a. Wheel lockup.
    b. Damage to steering axle.
    c. Poor traction on drive wheels.

82. Communication means:
    a. Talking with law enforcement officers.
    b. To communicate your intention to other motorists.
    c. To talk on the CB radio.

83. If you are convicted for driving under the influence while driving a commercial vehicle, and this is your first offence, you most likely will get:
    a. A probation period for 1 year.
    b. At least one year suspension of your CDL.
    c. A fine of $250.00

84. If you are stopped at a roadside rest area and found to have a BAC (Blood Alcohol Concentration) of 0.02 you will:
    a. Be place out of service for 72 hours.
    b. Be in deed trouble with your dispatcher.
    c. Be place out of service for 24 hours.

85. Which if the following statements about speed management is true?
    a. If you double your speed, stopping distance will double.
    b. Empty truck and loaded trucks will have the same stopping distance.
    c. If you double your speed, stopping distance will be increased by 4 times.

86. You are driving a long vehicle that makes wide turns. You want to make a left turn from Ocean Street onto Atlantic Street. There are two left turn lanes (marked A and B) on Ocean Street. You should:
    a. Use left turn lane A.
    b. Use left turn lane B.
    c. Start in left turn lane "A" and swing into left turn lane "B" just before entering the intersection.

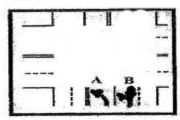

87. You are traveling down a long steep hill. You brakes get so hot that they failed. What should you do?
    a. Downshift and pump the brake pedal.
    b. Look for an escape ramp or escape route.
    c. Both of the above.

88. The center of gravity of a load:
    a. Should be kept as high as possible.
    b. Can make a vehicle more likely to tip over on curves if it is high.
    c. Is only a problem if the vehicle is overloaded.

89. To prevent a load from shifting, there should be at least one tiedown for every ___ feet of cargo.
    a. 10.
    b. 15.
    c. 20.

90. While driving, ice builds up on your wipers and they no longer clean the windshield. You should:
    a. Keep driving, and turn your defroster on.
    b. Keep driving and spray the windshield with washer fluid.
    c. Stop safely and fix the problem.

91. When the hydraulic brakes fail while you are driving, the system will not buildup pressure and the brake pedal will feel spongy or goes to the floor. What should you do?
    a. Pump the brake pedal to generate pressure.
    b. Push down the brake pedal as hard you can.
    c. Put the vehicle in neutral and set the parking brake.

92. Which may be a sign of tire failure?
    a. Wheels skidding.
    b. A loud hissing noise.
    c. Vibration.

93. To prevent brake fade you should:
    a. Coast downhill, which is not very steep.
    b. Apply constant hard pressure on the brakes while driving downhill.
    c. Select the gear, which will keep your vehicle to safe speed on a deep downgrade.

94. A full stop is required at railroad crossing when:
    a. There are no flagman, warning signal or gate at the crossing.
    b. The nature of a cargo makes a stop mandatory under the State of Federal regulations.
    c. The crossing is located in the city or town with a frequent train transit.

95. When driving at night you should use your low beams when oncoming vehicles is within of how many feet?
    a. 400
    b. 500
    c. 300

96. When driving through the work zone you should:
    a. Reduce your speed only if workers are close to the roadway
    b. Turn on your parking lights.
    c. Watch for sharp pavement drop off.

97. Backing of the commercial vehicle is:
    a. Always dangerous.
    b. Is not dangerous if you don't have to turn.
    c. Not dangerous if you have a helper.

98. When you are parked at the side of the road at night you must:
    a. Turn on your four-way to emergency flashers to warn others.
    b. Put out your emergency warning lights within 30 minutes.
    c. Use your taillights to give warning to other drivers.

99. You must stop on a hill or curve on a two-way road. How far should you place reflective triangles?
    a. As far back as necessary so others can see you.
    b. Within 200 feet behind you.
    c. Within 500 feet behind you.

100. Stab braking should not be used on vehicle with:
    a. Trailers.
    b. Antilock brakes.
    c. Hazardous materials.

101. Sometimes you need to leave a road to avoid a hazard or emergency. When you do so you should keep in mind, that:
    a. Most shoulders are not strong enough to support a heavy vehicle.
    b. You might be unable to reenter the road because of the gravel used on shoulders.
    c. It is less dangerous to drive onto the shoulders than to make a collision.

102. Which of the following is NOT a characteristic of the front tire failure?
    a. Vehicles fishtail.
    b. Steering wheel twisting.
    c. Cold steering.

103. Most skids
    a. Happen on ice.
    b. Do not happen with radial tires.
    c. Are caused by going too fast or trying to stop too quickly.

104. In a bad weather many car drivers tailgate large vehicles. What should you do?
    a. Increase your following distance.
    b. Lightly tap your brake to warn the tailgater to drop back.
    c. Speed up to distance yourself from the tailgater.

105. Which of the following systems should receive extra attention during winter weather inspection?
    a. Suspension.
    b. Exhaust.
    c. Steering.

106. What happens to tar on the road pavement during hot weather?
    a. Nothing.
    b. It becomes staining making tires stick to the road.
    c. It bleeds making the road surface slippery.

107. What is the best advice for driver when a heavy fog occurs?
   a. Do not drive too slowly or other drivers may hit you.
   b. Park the truck until the fog disappears.
   c. Alternate your own high beams to improve your vision.

108. In mounting driving you will have to use a lower gear to drive safely on a grade. Which of these does NOT affect your choice of gear?
   a. The length of the grade.
   b. The weight of the load.
   c. Tire tread's depth.

109. What should you do before driving in mountains?
   a. Know escape ramps location on your way.
   b. Unhook your steering axle brake.
   c. Carry the tire chains in your vehicle.

110. Escape ramps:
   a. Should be used by any driver who looses braking power.
   b. Are not designed for tractors-double trailers.
   c. Are designed to slow vehicles so they can get back on the road at the safe speed.

111. Which of these is true about notifying the authorities after an accident occurs?
   a. An exact location is not necessary just identify the road and the vehicles involved.
   b. You should notify authorities about an accident before doing anything else.
   c. If you have a cellular phone or CB radio you should notify the authorities before exiting the vehicle.

112. If you are not sure what to use to put out the hazardous material fire you should:
   a. Wait for fire fighters.
   b. Use water.
   c. Use dirt.

113. Which of these is NOT a danger of a rough acceleration?
   a. Mechanical damage.
   b. Tire damage.
   c. Damage of a coupling.

114. Which of these lights cannot be checked at the same time?
   a. Turn signals, taillights, and clearance lights.
   b. Turn signals, brake lights, and four-way flashers.
   c. Headlights, brake lights, and clearance lights.

115. You are inspecting hydraulic brakes. You should pump the brake pedal three times then apply firm pressure to the pedal for five seconds. If the breakes are working properly, the pedal should:
   a. Depress slightly.
   b. Sink to the floor.
   c. Not move.

116. Drivers of trucks and tractors-trailers with cargo must check that the cargo is well secured. within the first _____ miles of the trip.
   a. 25
   b. 10
   c. 50

117. When starting a bus on a level surface with good traction there is often no need for:
    a. Parking brakes.
    b. A tire check.
    c. Slow acceleration.

118. How the weight of the vehicle affects stopping distance?
    a. Fully loaded truck take longer to stop or the buses loaded with passengers take less distance than empty ones.
    b. If brakes work the same no matter what is the weight of the vehicle for both trucks and buses.
    c. Empty trucks take longer to stop than if loaded, but this is not normally the case for buses.

119. When you are starting to move up a hill from a stop:
    a. Release the parking brakes as you apply engine power.
    b. Engage the clutch and accelerate quickly.
    c. Keep the trailer brake hand valve applied until you reach 20 mph.

120. What is a true about using a heater?
    a. You must have at least one extra heater such as a mirror heater, battery pack heater or fuel tank heater when a temperature drops below freezing point.
    b. If you feel sleepy, warming up your cab with the heater will help you stay alert.
    c. When driving at winter weather you should check that the heater is working properly before starting.

121. Why a damage of exhaust system is a danger?
    a. Noise can damage the driver's ears.
    b. Poisonous fumes can enter into the cab or sleeping compartment.
    c. You can pollute the air with the exhaust smoke.

122. Which of these is NOT a danger when an automatic transmission is forced into a low gear at a high speed?
    a. A loss of engine braking effect.
    b. Damage to the transmission.
    c. A loss of steering control.

123. Perception distance is the distance your vehicle travels from the time:
    a. Your eyes see a hazard to the time your foot pushes to the brake pedal.
    b. The brain tells the foot to push the brake pedal to time the food responses.
    c. The eyes see a hazard to the brain knows that this is a hazard.

124. Extra care is needed to keep your vehicle centered in your lane because commercial vehicles:
    a. Require a lot of room to charge lane.
    b. Are often wider than other vehicle.
    c. Tend to sway from time to time.

125. Your should lightly apply your brakes to flash the brake lights if:
    a. You are about to exit the road and need to slow down.
    b. A police car is approaching you from the other direction.
    c. A driver tailgates you vehicle.

126. Merging to the road is safest if you:
    a. Wait for large enough gap in the traffic to enter the road.
    b. Bend over into the nearest lane so the other vehicle will give you room.
    c. Gain speed on the shoulder and then merge.

127. Which of these is NOT something you should do if your headlights are not working properly?
    a. Leave on your high beams.
    b. Clean your headlights.
    c. Adjust headlights.

128. Which of the statement about backing a heavy vehicle is NOT true?
    a. You should back and turn toward the driver's side whenever it is possible.
    b. You should use a helper and communicate with him with hand signals.
    c. Because you cannot see you should back slowly until you slightly bump into the dock.

129. The distance that you should look ahead of your vehicle while driving is about at low speed.
    a. 1 block.
    b. 2 blocks.
    c. 1/2 block.

130. Which of these is correct about emergency or evasive action?
    a. In order to turn quickly you must have a firm grip on the steering wheel.
    b. You can stop more quickly than you can turn to miss obstacles.
    c. Stopping is always the safest thing to do in a traffic emergency.

131. What does emergency braking mean?
    a. Pushing down the brake pedal as hard you can.
    b. Responding to a hazard by slowing the vehicle.
    c. Using the vehicles emergency brakes.

132. When driving in cold weather your tire tread should:
    a. Provide enough touch into steer and push the vehicle through snow.
    b. Be double the depth required in normal weather.
    c. Be checked every one hundred miles or every 2 hours.

133. Which of these is true about hauling of hazardous materials?
    a. Cylinders with compressed gases should be transported under covers if there is no label on them.
    b. Such a load should be marked with a four inches diamond shaped label on the containers.
    c. Such a load should be marked with a four inches circle red colored labels on the containers.

134. Which vehicle will have the most difficulties staying in its lane during strong wind?
    a. A double with an empty trailer.
    b. A tractor pulling a loaded flat bed trailer.
    c. A triple axle vehicle with cargo.

135. Why your vehicle speed naturally increases on a downgrade?
    a. Gravity.
    b. The engine runs smoother.
    c. Lack of traction.

136. During the vehicle inspection checking of _____ will NOT prevent a fire.
    a. Cargo ventilation.
    b. Battery fluid level.
    c. Electrical system isolation.

137. When it is necessary to learn how a fire extinguisher works?
    a. Before the fire happens.
    b. Only when the fire happens.
    c. Only when you are transporting flammable materials.

138. What is the most important reason to inspect your truck or bus?
    a. Safety.
    b. To avoid being cited.
    c. It's the law.

139. You are checking your steering and exhaust system in a pre-trip inspection. Which of these problems, if found, should be fixed before the vehicle is driven:
   a. Steering wheel play more then 10 degrees (2 inches on 20 inches steering wheel).
   b. Oil on a tire rod.
   c. If a gray smoke coming out from the exhaust pipe.

140. Convex (curved) mirrors:
   a. Make objects appear closer than they really are.
   b. Make objects appear larger than they really are.
   c. They show the wider area than flat mirrors show.

141. Why it is important to shift gears correctly?
   a. To keep control of the vehicle.
   b. To keep the engine warm.
   c. To keep the engine oil flowing.

142. What three distances build up the total stopping distance of your truck or bus?
   a. Attention distance, reaction distance and slowing distance.
   b. Respond distance, observation distance, and braking distance.
   c. Perception distance, reaction distance and braking distance.

143. Which of these actions are NOT recommended for a left turn?
   a. Start at the inside lane and swing right as you turn.
   b. Use a right hand turn lane if there are two turning lanes.
   c. Start your turn in the center of the intersection.

144. When you passing the other vehicle, pedestrian or bicycle you should assume that:
   a. They may be moving to your traffic lane.
   b. They know you are to pass
   c. They see your vehicle.

145. In your mirror you see a car approaching from the rear. The next time you check your mirror you do not see the car. If you wish to change the lane, you should:
   a. Wait to change lane until you are sure that car is not in your blind spot.
   b. Ease to another lane very slowly so cars, which are besides of you can get out of your way.
   c. Assume that car left the road and change the lane.

146. Which of these is the proper signal to change lane?
   a. Signal early and change lane slowly and smoothly.
   b. Signal before the change and move over quickly.
   c. Signal after you begin change and cross over slowly.

147. You are driving in the area with a few street lights. If you cannot see well with your headlights, which of the actions may help:
   a. Find another route that is better lit even if it is out of your way.
   b. Turn your interior lights on and adjust your instrument lights.
   c. Use your high beams when legal and keep your interior lights off.

148. Most serious skid results from:
   a. Driving to fast for conditions.
   b. Turning too sharply.
   c. An uneven load.

149. What should be true about other drivers:
   a. Mail or delivery trucks are professionals and do not pose a hazard.
   b. Drivers who use turn signals always should be trusted to turn to direction, which they indicate.
   c. Short term or daily rental truck drivers are often not used to the limited vision and posed the hazard.

150. What is true about bad weather and driving conditions?
   a. **When the temperature drops, the bridges freeze before the road.**
   b. The road is more slippery when the rain continues than when rain begins.
   c. Driving conditions became more dangerous when temperature arises above freezing.

151. Which of these statements about hazard of vehicle fire is true?
   a. **Poor cargo ventilation may cause cargo to catch on fire.**
   b. Carrying a fully charged fire extinguisher may prevent a fire.
   c. Underinflated tire do not cause a vehicle fire.

152. You should wear a seat belt in a moving vehicle:
   a. Only when you are driving.
   b. **All the time.**
   c. Only when you are on a highway.

153. Which of these items is NOT checked for a pre-trip inspection?
   a. Whatever all lights are working.
   b. **Amount of fuel on a vehicle.**
   c. Cargo securement.

154. Which of the statements about pre trip inspection is true?
   a. When you park on a street, you should walk so you face away from an oncoming traffic.
   b. Leave key in the ignition so you do not loose it when you are under the truck.
   c. **If you need to tilt a cab, secure loose things so that they could not fall or break anything.**

155. Can state inspectors inspect your truck or bus?
   a. No
   b. Yes, but cannot put you out of service.
   c. **Yes and they can put you out of service if unsafe.**

156. Which of these statements about cargo loading is true?
   a. **A state law dictates legal weight limit.**
   b. If cargo is loaded by the shipper a driver is not responsible for its load.
   c. The legal maximum weight allowed by the state is considered safe for all driving conditions.

157. Which of these is not required knowledge of driver needed a hazardous material endorsement?
   a. **Basic chemistry.**
   b. Which products can be loaded together.
   c. When to use the placards.

158. To determine blood alcohol concentration level for a person it is necessary to know:
   a. **How much a person weights.**
   b. How often a person drinks alcohol.
   c. How old is a person.

159. Implied consent means:
   a. You are giving your consent to inspect your vehicle for alcohol.
   b. If is understood that you may drink alcohol now and then.
   c. **You are given your consent to be tested for alcohol in your blood.**

160. The engine brake effect is greater when the engine is governed RPM and the transmission is on a gear.
   a. Below, higher.
   b. **Near, lower.**
   c. Above, lower.

161. You are driving a 40 feet vehicle at 55 mph. The road is dry and visibility is good. What is a least amount of space that you need to have in front of your vehicle?
    a. 4 seconds.
    b. 5 seconds.
    c. 6 seconds.

162. What should you do if a car coming toward you at night keeps its high beams on?
    a. Flash your high beams quickly at the other driver.
    b. Look to the right lane or edge markings of the road.
    c. Slow down and look straight ahead in your lane.

163. If you must stop into the oncoming lane as you make a turn, you should:
    a. Watch for an oncoming traffic.
    b. Complete your turn without stopping.
    c. Back to allow the oncoming traffic to pass.

164. Which of these is true about driving in a tunnel?
    a. Emergency flashers are required by law.
    b. Headlights are required by law.
    c. There may be strong winds when exiting.

165. You should use your horn when:
    a. If it helps to avoid a crash.
    b. A car is in your way.
    c. You want to change a lane.

166. The tread depth on a front steering wheels tires should be:
    a. Not less than 4/32 inch.
    b. More than 6/32 inch.
    c. Not less than 2/32 inch.

167. Your vehicle will be put out of service if or more leaves in any leaf spring are missing.
    a. 1/4
    b. 1/3
    c. 1/2

168. Brake drums (or discs) must NOT have cracks longer than the width of the friction area.
    a. 1/2
    b. 1/3
    c. 1/10

169. A hazard:
    a. Is any road condition or other road user that is possible danger.
    b. Cannot turn into emergency.
    c. Does not need to be seen.

170. You are driving a heavy vehicle. You must exit a highway using an off-ramp that curves downhill. You should:
    a. Slow to the posted speed limit for off-ramp.
    b. Slow down to 5 mph below the posted limit.
    c. Slow down to 15 mph below the posted speed limit.

171. Which of these rigs have more chances to "off-track" while making turn?
    a. Tractor with 45-fee trailer.
    b. Tractor with two 27-feet trailer.
    c. 53-feet straight truck.

172. How much space in front of you is needed while driving on a highway?
 a. 1 Second for each 10 feed of vehicle length.
 b. 1 Second for each 20 feed of vehicle length.
 c. 1 Second for each 30 feed of vehicle length.

173. Medicine used to treat the common cold:
 a. Should only be used when driving at daytime
 b. Often makes you sleepy and should not be used while driving.
 c. May still be used while driving if you use half of a regular dose.

174. Which of these you should NOT do in an emergency situation?
 a. You should brake in a way that keeps your vehicle in a straight line.
 b. It is not important how you brake in an emergency situation.
 c. You should avoid using the brakes until your speed is down to 40 mph.

175. The primary cause of fatal crashes is:
 a. Driving at night.
 b. Driving while eating.
 c. Driving too fast.

176. A car suddenly cuts in front of you, creating a hazard. Which of these actions should you NOT take?
 a. Honk your horn and stay close behind the car.
 b. Signal and change lanes to avoid hazard.
 c. Slow down to prevent a crash.

177. What should you do when you see a hazard in the roadway ahead of you?
 a. Steer around it and get back in your lane.
 b. Stop quickly and pull to the side of the road.
 c. Use your four way flashers or brake lights to warn others.

178. If your brakes fail on a downgrade, you must first:
 a. Look outside your vehicle for another means of slowing you.
 b. Hit some object in order to stop your vehicle.
 c. Find an escape ramp in order to exit roadway.

179. You should always turn on your emergency four-way flashers when you:
 a. Drive through the mountains.
 b. Park on the side of the road.
 c. Cross railway tracks.

180. Should brake adjustment be checked often?
 a. It depends on how new the brakes are.
 b. No because the other brakes will make up for the air brakes when they are out of adjustment.
 c. Yes, because the brakes can get out of adjustment when they are used a lot.

181. Which of these is true about mirror adjusting?
 a. You should adjust your mirrors before starting the trip.
 b. You should adjust your mirrors while you are driving.
 c. The mirrors could be adjusted correctly even if the trailer is not straight.

182. When you are driving on a snow packed road, you should reduce your speed by:
 a. 1/3
 b. 1/4
 c. 1/2

183. The bridge formula:

    a. Permits less maximum axle weight for the axles that are close together.

    b. Permits less maximum axle weight for the axles that are far apart.

    c. Permits the same maximum axle weight for any axle.

184. Which of these is true about hours of service?

    a. After you have reached a thousand hours of service you'll be exempt a service regulation.

    b. You should allow enough hours to rest.

    c. You have to make a break after every two hours of driving.

185. Which of these is true about the use of drugs while driving?

    a. Prescription or non-prescription drugs are allowed at any time of driving.

    b. Use of amphetamine is allowed if you are using this drug to stay alert.

    c. Prescription drugs are allowed-if a doctor says they will not affect the driving ability.

186. Which of these is true about proper use of a steering wheel?

    a. If you do not hold a wheel with both hands it could pull away from you.

    b. If you have reached a cruising speed on a highway you can drive with one you

    c. Only with an attempt of a difficult turn use both hands on the wheel.

187. When helper needs to be used to back your vehicle?

    a. Only if you need to park.

    b. Whenever you have to back.

    c. Only if you have a trailer on your vehicle.

188. To avoid an accident you moved to the shoulder. To return to the road:

    a. Ride on shoulder to the next exit and then re-enter road.

    b. Using mirrors and turn signals turn sharply to get back to the road.

    c. Using mirrors and turn signals return when the road is clear.

189. Which of these would NOT help if windshield covered with ice?

    a. Brush.

    b. Scraper.

    c. Defroster.

190. Heavy vehicles often move slower than others. Which of these is NOT a good rule to follow while driving a heavy vehicle?

    a. Stay on a right side of the road.

    b. Use four-way flashers if it is legal in your state.

    c. Signal other drivers when it is safe to pass you.

191. Why tourists may be hazard?

    a. They drive rented cars.

    b. They may move slowly, unexpectedly lanes or stop.

    c. Police do not fine them.

192. What keep as engine cool in a hot weather driving?

    a. Enough engine oil level.

    b. Air conditioner use.

    c. High speed driving in order to put more air to the radiator.

193. Cargo inspection.

    a. Is most often not the responsibility of the driver.

    b. Should be performed after every break you take while driving.

    c. Are needed only if hazardous materials are being hauled.

194. A vehicle is loaded with very little weight on the drive axle. What may happen?
   a. **Poor traction.**
   b. Damage to driver axle tires.
   c. Better handling.

195. If you vehicle catches fire while you are driving, you should:
   a. **Park in a open area.**
   b. Park where a building or trees shelter you vehicle from the wind.
   c. Increase your speed to put the flames.

196. Turn signals should be used:' -
   a. **At least 100 feet before turning or changing lane.**
   b. At least 150 feet before turning or changing lane.
   c. At least 200 feet before turning or changing lane.

197. Containerized loads:
   a. Are not require to be inspected by a driver.
   b. Should be supplied with their own tiedown devices or locks.
   c. **Generally are used when freight is carried part way by rail or ship.**

198. When driving a commercial vehicle with a height over 13 feet, you should:
   a. Not worry about height clearance as long as you stay on state or federal highways.
   b. Assume all clearances are high enough.
   c. **Stop and make sure that a clearance is high enough.**

199. When should you test your parking brakes?
   a. While moving at a very low speed.
   b. **While the vehicle is parked.**
   c. When backing.

200. When going down a long steep downgrade you should always:
   a. **Use the braking effect of the engine:**
   b. Use controlled braking.
   c. Brake when you exceed safe speed by 5 mph.

201. Controlled Braking is:
   a. Slamming on the brakes hard and making wheels lock up.
   b. Squeezing the brakes firmly without locking them up.
   c. **Pressing Brakes until wheel lock-up occurs, releasing and then reapplying.**

202. Which of these is not a brake check you normally do during your walk-around inspection?
   a. **Brake adjustment**
   b. Conditions of hoses.
   c. Hydraulic brake cylinders leaks.

203. One can recognize hazardous materials by looking on the container:
   a. **Labels.**
   b. Shapes.
   c. Covers.

204. Which of these is not type of retarders.
   a. Electric.
   b. Hydraulic.
   c. **Robotic.**

205. Truck and buses are subjects of certain law regulations and inspections. Which of these is true?

    a. County and city laws do not apply to trucks and buses engaged into interstate commerce.

    b. Federal regulations apply only to trucks and buses driven at least 50 mph.

    c. Laws and restrictions can vary from place to place.

206. When approaching a bridge in a two-lane road you should:

    a. Drive in the center of the bridge.

    b. Check the weight limit of the bridge.

    c. Slow down to 25 mph on the bridge.

207. Which of the statement is true?

    a. Most people are more alert at night than during the day.

    b. Most hazards are easier to see at night than during the day.

    c. Many heavy vehicles accidents occur between midnight and 6 am.

208. A space to the _____ your vehicle is most important to manage.

    a. Back of.

    b. Front of

    c. To the side of.

209. Your brake can get wet when you are driving through the heavy rain. What can happen if the brakes are applied?

    a. Hydroplaning.

    b. Extensive brake wear.

    c. Trailer jack-knife.

210. Which of the statement about an inspection of the suspension is true?

    a. Distorted springs are safe as long as they are not broken.

    b. Axels' mounts should be checked at each point they are secured on the vehicle frame and axels.

    c. Suspension components should be checked at all axels except for the following unit.

211. You are checking your brakes and suspension system for a pre-trip inspection. Which of these statement is true?

    a. Just one missing leaf in a leaf spring is not dangerous.

    b. Spring hangers that are cracked but still tight are not dangerous.

    c. Brake shoes should not have oil, grease or brake fluid on them.

212. You do not have Hazardous materials endorsement in your commercial driver license. You can drive a vehicle hauling hazardous materials when:

    a. The load of the hazardous materials is 26 pounds or less.

    b. The vehicle does not require placards.

    c. The person who has Hazmat endorsement drives with you.

213. If you have convicted of driving a commercial vehicle under influence of alcohol or drug you will loose your CDL for:

    a. 6 months.

    b. 1 year.

    c. 2 years.

214. Which of these is true about hazardous materials:

    a. All hazardous materials present health and safety danger.

    b. Any truck carrying any amount of hazardous materials must have placards.

    c. Any public road allow trucks, carrying hazardous materials if they are loaded correctly.

215. You will be placed out of service for 24 hours if you blood alcohol concentration (BAC) is at least:

    a. 0.02.

    b. 0.04.

    c. Any detectable amount.

216. What does emergency braking mean?
   a. Pushing down the brake pedal as hard as you can.
   b. Responding to a hazard by slowing the vehicle.
   c. Using the vehicle emergency brakes.

217. You should try park so that:
   a. You can pull forward when you leave.
   b. Park along curb next to other vehicle.
   c. That you vehicle is parked by tree

218. Which of these statements is true about using engine brake?
   a. You should use the engine brakes as a main way to control you speed.
   b. Increasing use of the engine brake prevents extra friction between the brake shoes apart of the drum.
   c. The use of the brakes on downgrade add to the braking effect of the engine.

219. After starting the engine;
   a. The coolant temperature gauge should be read right to normal.
   b. The oil pressure gauge should be read right to normal.
   c. The engine oil temperature gauge should be read right to normal.

220. Whenever you double your speed your vehicle has about how many times of destructive power if it crashes?
   a. 2
   b. 3
   c. 4

221. If you do not have a C-B radio what is the procedure you should do on the accident scene?
   a. Protect the area.
   b. Notify the authority.
   c. Care for the injured person.

222. If you have a heavy load that slowing you down on an upgrade you should:
   a. Shifting to the lower gear.
   b. Exit the road until traffic is lighter.
   c. Drive on a shoulder that the others can pass your vehicle.

223. You should signal continuously while turning because:
   a. You need both hands on the wheel to turn safety.
   b. It is illegal to turn off your signal before completing the turn.
   c. Most vehicle have self-canceling signals.

224. Which of these should be tested on the vehicle to stop?
   a. Service brake.
   b. Parking brake.
   c. Hydraulic brake.

225. Which of these about alcohol is NOT true?
   a. Alcohol goes directly from the stomach to the blood stream.
   b. Drinker can control how fast his body absorbs alcohol he gets.
   c. SAC is determined by how fast you drink, how much you drink and how much you eat.

226. Over weight, over sized loads:
   a. Require special permits.
   b. Can only be driver at the daylight.
   c. Must be accompanied by the police.

227. Which of the statement about braking is true?
   a. **The heavier vehicle is or the faster it is moving, the more heat the brakes have to absorb to stop it.**
   b. Brake responding is very quickly when the vehicle is moving very fast.
   c. Brake face is not caused by heat.

228. Which of these pieces of emergency equipment should always be carried in your vehicle?
   a. Tire repair kit.
   b. Fist aid kit.
   c. **Warning devices for parking vehicle.**

229. In a mountain driving you should go slow for safety. Which of these is the most important?
   a. **Weight of the vehicle.**
   b. Tire tread type.
   c. Depth of the tread.

230. You must keep the papers about hauling hazardous materials:
   a. Under the driver seat.
   b. **In the pouch of the driver door.**
   c. In the glove compartment, which must be working.

231. Which of the statements is true about rear drive wheel braking skid?
   a. Locked wheels usually have more traction that rolling wheels.
   b. Front wheels slide sideway to try to catch up with the rear wheels.
   c. **On a vehicle with a trailer the trailer can push the towing vehicle sideways.**

232. The best drivers are who watch and prepare for hazard. This is called the driving:
   a. Offensive.
   b. **Defensive.**
   c. Objective

233. Which of these is true about commercial vehicle habit of swinging wide on turns?
   a. **Off-tracking.**
   b. Wide rounding.
   c. Side winding.

234. You may hang up on a railroad tracks if:
   a. If you cross the double tracks to slowly.
   b. **The track have a steep approach.**
   c. You try to shift gear when crossing.

235. Which of these is true about radiator shutters and the winterfront during the winter driving?
   a. The winter front should be closed tightly.
   b. **Ice should be removed from the radiator shutter.**
   c. The engine may overheat if winterfront left open.

236. What kind of optional equipment (except tire wrench) could be in your vehicle?
   a. Fully charged fire extinguisher.
   b. Set of warning device.
   c. **Battery charger.**

237. Which of these do not provide extra gears on some trucks?
   a. **Automatic transmission.**
   b. Auxiliary transmission.
   c. Multi-speed rear axles.

238. Which of these is true about tire pressure?
   a. **Air pressure in tires increases with the temperature.**
   b. You do not have to check the hot tires, because the tire is not to blow out.
   c. The pressure is not to be checked during the trip if it passed the pre-trip inspection.

239. What should you do if are unsure whether you have enough overhead clearance?
   a. Slow down slightly and try to drive under object.
   b. **Find another route that will not require driving under the object.**
   c. Estimate the height of topped overhead object if it is not posted.

240. What should you do when vehicle hydroplanes?
   a. Start stab braking.
   b. **Release accelerator.**
   c. Accelerate slightly.

241. Which of these is true about tires and hot weather?
   a. **You should check pressure before driving.**
   b. If a tire is too hot to touch, you should drive on it to cool it off.
   c. A small amount of air could be let out but air pressure remains stable.

242. You drive through the heavy rain or snow. You con hardly see what is going on outside. You can let the other drivers know about you by:
   a. Blowing your horn.
   b. Turning on inside cab lights.
   c. **Turning on the lower beam headlights.**

Air Brake Test

1. The application Pressure Gauge shows how much air pressure you.
    a. Have in the air tanks.
    b. **Are applying to the brakes.**
    c. Have in a modulating control valve.

2. The spring brakes use on the chambers in a straight truck will bring you to a stop when air pressure drop below _____ psi.
    a. **20**
    b. 60
    c. 100

3. Some air brake systems have an alcohol evaporator. What may happen if you don't keep the proper level of an alcohol?
    a. The S-cam may not take back when you release the brake.
    b. **Ice may form in the air storage tank and cause a brake failure.**
    c. Ice may form on the brake drums and wear them out.

4. Your truck or bus has a dual air brake system. If a low air pressure warning comes on for only one system, what should you do?
    a. **Bring your vehicle to a complete stop right away and safely park. Continue after the system is fixed.**
    b. Reduce your speed, and test the remaining system while under way.
    c. Reduce your speed and drive to nearest garage for repair.

5. Why drain water from compressor air tank?
    a. Water low boiling point reduces braking power.
    b. **Water can freeze in cold weather and cause brake failure.**
    c. Water cools the compress too much.

6. The Safety valve is set automatically when pressure is.
    a. 50
    b. 100
    c. **150**

7. Your truck has a dual air system and one of the systems loses its pressure. What will happen?
    a. Brake drums will be fully pressurized.
    b. The manual slack adjusters of the S-cam brakes will not be set properly.
    c. **Either the front or back brake will not be fully operational.**

8. Parking or emergency brakes of trucks and buses can be legally held on by _____ pressure.
    a. **Spring.**
    b. Air
    c. Fluid.

9. If your truck or bus has dual parking control valves, you can use pressure from a separate tank to:
    a. Balance the service brakes system when you are parked.
    b. Stay parked twice as long without using up service air.
    c. **Release the spring emergency/parking brakes to move a short distance.**

10. If your truck has a properly functioning dual brake system and minimum size air tank the air pressure should build up from 85 to 100 psi within how many seconds?
    a. 60
    b. 30
    c. **45**

11. How should you check that your service brakes are working properly?
    a. Park on slight grade, drain of air pressure brake, set parking brakes and check to the movement.
    b. Park on a level ground, chock the wheels, engage the parking brakes when you have the correct amount of air pressure to do so and shut the engine off.
    c. **Park on level ground, wait until normal air pressure is reached, release the parking brake and move forward slowly at about 5 mph. Then apply the brakes firmly using your brake pedal.**

12. A Straight truck or bus air brake systems should not leak at the rate of more than _____ psi per minute with the engine off and the brake released
    a. 1.
    b. 2.
    c. 3.

13. During normal driving, spring brakes are usually held back by:
    a. Bolts or clamps.
    b. Air pressure.
    c. Spring pressure.

14. The air compressor stops pumping air at what psi?
    a. 100
    b. 125
    c. 150

15. The driver must be able to see low air pressure warning which come on before pressure in the service air tank falls bellow _____ psi.
    a. 40
    b. 60
    c. 80

16. Excessive use of the service brakes results in overheating which can lead to:
    a. Proper adjustment of S-cam.
    b. Increase contact between the brake drums and linings.
    c. Expansion of the brake drums.

17. The most common type of foundation brake found on heavy vehicles is the:
    a. Wedge drums.
    b. S-cam drum.
    c. Disc.

18. If you must make and emergency stop, you should brake so you:
    a. Use the hand brake before the brake pedal.
    b. Can steer and so you vehicle stays in straight line.
    c. Use the full power of the brakes to lock them.

19. Your Truck or bus has a dual air brake system. If a low air pressure warning comes on for only one system, what should you do?
    a. Reduce your speed and drive to the nearest garage for repairs.
    b. Reduce you speed and drive to the nearest garage for repairs.
    c. Stop right away and safety park. Continue only after the system is fixed.

20. If your vehicle has an alcohol evaporator, every day during cold weather you should:
    a. Check and fill the alcohol level.
    b. Change the alcohol from a new bottle
    c. Check the oil for alcohol content.

21. The air loss rate for a straight truck or bus with the engine off and the brakes on should not be more than:
    a. 1 psi in 30 seconds.
    b. 2 psi in 45 seconds.
    c. 3 psi in one minute.

22. The driver must be able to see low air pressure warning which come on before pressure in the service air tank falls bellow _____ psi.
    a. 40
    b. 60
    c. 80

23. The braking power of the spring brakes:
    a. Is not affected by the condition of the service brakes:
    b. **Depends on the service brakes being in adjustment.**
    c. Increases when the service brakes are hot.

24. The air brake lag distance at 55 mph on dry pavement adds about _____ feet.
    a. 12 feet.
    b. **32 feet.**
    c. 52 feet.

25. Total stopping distance for air brakes is longer than for hydraulic brakes to _____ distance.
    a. **Brake lag**
    b. Reaction.
    c. Effective braking.

26. It is accepted that too much heat caused by using your brakes too often can also cause:
    a. Modulated control valve to wear out.
    b. Brake linings to split up.
    c. **Brake to fade or fail.**

27. Repeatedly partially releasing and pressing the brakes too often can also cause:
    a. **A loss of braking air pressure.**
    b. A build up of brake air pressure.
    c. No change of brake air pressure.

28. The brake system that applies and releases the brakes when the driver uses the brake pedal is the _____ brake system.
    a. Emergency.
    b. **Service.**
    c. Parking.

29. A slack adjuster's free play needs to be adjusted if it is more than about _____ how many inches when you pull hard on it?
    a. 1/4 inch
    b. 1/2 inch
    c. **1 inch**

30. An air brake system is fully charged at what psi?
    a. 75
    b. 100
    c. **125**

31. Your truck or bus has a dual air bake system. If a low air pressure warning comes on for only system, what should you do?
    a. **Bring your vehicle to a complete stop right away and safely park. Continue after the system is fixed.**
    b. Reduce your speed, and test the remaining system while under way.
    c. Reduce your speed and drive to nearest garage for repair.

32. The air brake pedal in an air brake system:
    a. Control the speed of the air compressor.
    b. **Control the air pressure applied to put on the brake.**
    c. Is connected to slack adjusters by a series of rods and linkages.

33. The S-cam:
    a. Controls the flow air to each of the brake chambers.
    b. Pulls the brake shoes away from the drum and allow the wheel to roll freely.
    c. **Forces the brake shoes against the inside of the brake drum.**

34. Under normal condition in order to engage the parking brakes driver:
    a. Turn off the engine.
    b. **Let the air out of air brake system.**
    c. Be sure air brakes system is fully pressurized.

35. All Air equipped vehicle have:
    a. **A supply pressure gauge.**
    b. A air usage gauge.
    c. A backup hydraulic system.

36. With air brake vehicles, the parking brakes should be used.
    a. **Whenever you leave the vehicle unattended.**
    b. As little as possible.
    c. Only during pre-trip inspections.

37. A straight or bus air brake system should not leak at the rate of more than _____ psi per minute with the engine off and the brakes released.
    a. 1.
    b. 3.
    c. **2.**

38. Which of these is not a proper time to apply the brakes?
    a. **To brake vehicle very hard, in other word when coming down the steep grade.**
    b. To use parking brake if you park for less than 1 hour.
    c. If you are going to use the parking brakes you need to make sure that they will hold the vehicle.

39. With air brake vehicle, the parking brakes should be used :
    a. As little as possible.
    b. **Any time when vehicle is parked.**
    c. To hold your speed when going downhill

40. Why should you drain the water from compressed air tanks?
    a. Water low boiling point reduces braking power.
    b. **Water can freeze in cold weather and cause brake failure.**
    c. To keep from fowling the air compressor oil.

41. If the spring brake are on, when should you press the brake pedal?
    a. Only when driving downhill.
    b. Only on the slippery road.
    c. **Never.**

42. To check the free play of manual slack S-cam brakes, you should park on:
    a. **Level ground, chock the wheels and release the parking brakes.**
    b. Level ground and apply the parking brakes, then apply service brakes.
    c. Level ground and drain off air pressure before checking the adjustment.

43. Excessive heat cause by using your brakes too often can cause:
    a. Modulated control valve to wear out.
    b. Brake linings to split up.
    c. **Brake to fade or fail.**

44. If you must make an emergency stop, you should brake so you:
    a. Can steer hard while braking hard
    b. **Can steer and so your vehicle stays in a straight line.**
    c. Use the hand brake first.

56. When brakes are applied the brake shoes will align to press against the ____.
    a. **Brake drum or disc.**
    b. Slack adjuster.
    c. S-cam.

57. Why should you drain water from compressed air tanks?
    a. Water low boiling point reduces braking power.
    b. **Water can freeze in cold weather and cause brake failure.**
    c. To keep heat from air compressor oil.

58. If you must make an emergency stop you should brake so you:
    a. Use the hand brake before the brake pedal.
    b. **Can steer and so your vehicle stays in a straight line.**
    c. Use the full power of the brake to lock them.

59. The supply pressure gauge shows how much pressure:
    a. **Is in the air tanks.**
    b. You have used in the trip.
    c. Is going to the brake chamber.

60. The supply pressure gauge shows much pressure:
    a. **Is in the air tanks.**
    b. Is in the Tractor brake lines.
    c. Is in the Trailer brake lines.

61. The braking power of the spring brake:
    a. **Depends if the service brakes are in adjustment.**
    b. Is not affected by the condition of the service brakes.
    c. Can only be tested by highly-trained brake service people.

62. Your brakes are fading when:
    a. **You have pushed harder on brake pedal to control your speed on a downgrade.**
    b. Less pressure is needed on the brake pedal for each stop.
    c. The brake pedal feels spongy when you apply pressure.

63. If your vehicle has an alcohol evaporator, it is there to:
    a. Eliminate the need for daily tank draining.
    b. Boost tank pressure the same way that turbochargers boost engine.
    c. **When air is pumped into the air tanks.**

64. The air compressor governor controls:
    a. The speed of the air compressor
    b. Air pressure applied to the air brakes.
    c. **When air is pumped into the air tanks.**

65. Modern air brake systems combine three different systems. They are the service, the parking and the _____ brakes.
    a. **Emergency.**
    b. Foot.
    c. Drum.

66. If you do not have automatic tank drains, how often should you drain the oil and water from the bottom of compressed air storage tanks.
    a. After every four hours of service.
    b. **At the end of each day of driving.**
    c. Once a week.

67. The proper use of the brakes when going down a long steep grade after selecting a proper gear is to brake until speed is about _____ mph below the posted speed for your safety and release your parking brake.
    a. 5 mph.
    b. 15 mph.
    c. 10 mph.

68. In ideal conditions a truck or bus with an air brake going 55 mph would require a stopping distance of how many feet?
    a. Less than 100 feet.
    b. More than 300 feet.
    c. From 100 to 300 feet.

69. When is it OK to leave your truck unattended without applying parking brakes and choking the wheel?
    a. Never.
    b. If you are only away for a few minutes.
    c. If you are conducting a pre-trip inspection.

70. The stop light switch
    a. Tells you when the air brake system is at low air pressure.
    b. Tells you when you need to use your emergency brakes.
    c. Turns on your brake lights to warn drivers behind you.

71. It is not safe to drive a vehicle that has brake drums with cracks that are longer than _____ of the width of the frictions area
    a. 1/2
    b. 1/4
    c. 1/8

72. To test air service you should
    a. Stop the vehicle brake in a low gear, the depress.
    b. Brake firmly while slowly moving forward.
    c. Brake slowly while slowly moving forward.

73. If you are driving down to the steep downgrade and you have reached the speed of 40 mph, you should apply the service brake until your speed drops to _____ mph.
    a. 25
    b. 30
    c. 35

74. Front brake limiting valves are found on:
    a. Older vehicles made before 1975.
    b. New imports vehicles only.
    c. School buses.

Combination Test

1. Where should the tractor be when you inspect landing gear after uncoupling the trailer?
   - **a. With the tractor frame under the trailer.**
   - b. Completely cleared from the trailer.
   - c. With the fifth wheel directly beneath the kingpin

2. While driving other vehicle under good condition you should allow at least one second between your vehicle and vehicle ahead for each _____ (how many) feet of vehicle length?
   - a. 10
   - b. 20
   - c. 30

3. There are two things that a driver can do to prevent a rollover. They are (1) keep the cargo as close to the ground as possible; and (2)
   - a. Make sure that the brakes are properly adjusted.
   - b. Keep both hands firmly on the steering wheel.
   - **c. Go slow around turns.**

4. The air brake leakage rate for a combination vehicle (engine off, brakes off) should be less than psi per minute.
   - a. 1/2.
   - b. 2.
   - **c. 3.**

5. The safest way to make turn without entering another traffic lane is:
   - a. You should turn wide before you start the turn.
   - **b. You should turn wide as you complete the turn.**
   - c. You should not make a turn and move to another place where you can make a turn without crossing other lane.

6. The higher the center of gravity of your truck, the;
   - a. Easier to turn around the corner.
   - b. More stable while turning.
   - **c. Easier to turn over.**

7. If the service line comes apart while you are driving a combination vehicle but the emergency line stays together, what will happen right away?
   - a. The trailer's tank will exhaust through the open line.
   - b. The emergency trailer brakes will come on.
   - **c. Nothing is likely to happen until you try to apply the brakes.**

8. Glad hand are usually connecting which of these?
   - a. Electric lines from the tractor to trailer.
   - b. Kingpin from the trailer to the locking jaws of the fifth wheel.
   - **c. Service and emergency air lines from the vehicle to the trailer.**

9. A driver crosses the air lines when hooking up to and old trailer. What will happen?
   - a. the hand valve will apply the tractor brakes instead of the trailer brakes.
   - **b. If the trailer has no spring brakes, you could drive away but you wouldn't have trailer brakes.**
   - c. The brake light will come on when the brake pedal is pressed.

10. The hand valve should be used:
    - a. Only with a foot brake.
    - **b. To test the trailer brakes.**
    - c. As a parking brake.

11. When driving a set of doubles it is necessary to close which shut-off valve in the last trailer.

    a. Front

    b. Middle section.

    c. Back.

12. If the service line comes apart while you are driving a combination vehicle but the emergency line stays together, what will happen right away?

    a. The trailer's tank will exhaust through the open line

    b. The emergency trailer brakes will come on.

    c. Nothing is likely to happen until you try to apply the brakes.

13. You are about to back your tractor under a semitrailer. The trailer is at the right height when the:

    a. Kingpin is about 1 1/4 inches about the fifth wheel.

    b. End of the kingpin is even with the top of the fifth wheel.

    c. Trailer will be lifted slightly when the tractor backs under it.

14. Your emergency air line breaks or gets pulled apart while you are driving. The loss of pressure will cause the:

    a. Air compressor to unload instead of pumping air.

    b. Emergency trailer brakes to come on.

    c. Trailer supply valve to open.

15. If the brakes are not released when you pushed the trailer air supply valve you should.

    a. Check air line connection.

    b. Cross the airlines.

    c. Check electrical cable.

16. Air brake equipped trailers made before 1975;

    a. Often do not have spring brakes.

    b. Usually need a glad hand converter.

    c. Cannot be legally operated on interstate highways.

17. There are two things that a driver can do to prevent a rollover. They are: (1) for slow around turns; and (2)

    a. Keep both hands firmly on the steering wheel.

    b. Keep the cargo as close to the ground as possible.

    c. Make sure that the brakes are properly balanced.

18. After connecting the air lines but before backing under the trailer you should:

    a. Supply air to the trailer system, then pull out the supply knob.

    b. Make sure that the trailer brakes are off.

    c. Walk around the rig to be sure that it is clear.

19. Which part of the kingpin should the locking jaws close around?

    a. The shank.

    b. The head.

    c. The base.

20. How much space should be allowed between upper and lower fifth wheel after coupling?

    a. 1/4 inch.

    b. Just enough to sit on.

    c. Nothing.

21. You have pushed the trailer air supply valve. You should not back a tractor under a trailer until the whole air system is:

    a. Empty.

    b. At normal pressure.

    c. Between 60 and 80 psi.

22. You are coupling tractor to a semitrailer. You have connected the airlines. Before backing under the trailer you should:
    a. Supply air to the trailer system, then pull out the air supply knob.
    b. Pull ahead to test the glad hands connections.
    c. Make sure that the trailer brakes are off.

23. You are coupling a tractor to a semitrailer and have backed up but are not under it. What should you hook up before backing under?
    a. The emergency and service air lines.
    b. The electrical service cable.
    c. Nothing. Back up and lock the fifth wheel.

24. Tractor with _____ trailer requires the shortest amount of stopping distance.
    a. Empty.
    b. Partly loaded.
    c. Fully loaded.

25. There are two thing that a driver can do to prevent a rollover. They are (1) keep the cargo as close to the ground as possible; and (2):
    a. Make sure that the brakes are properly adjusted.
    b. Keep both hands firmly on the steering wheel.
    c. Go slow around turns.

26. After you have coupled the trailer you should have to raise the landing gear by using:
    a. Low gear.
    b. Intermediate.
    c. High gear.

27. You supply air to the trailer tanks by:
    a. Pushing in the trailer air supply valve.
    b. Pulling out the trailer air supply valve.
    c. Connecting the service line glad hands.

28. There are two things that a driver can do to prevent a rollover. They are (1) go slow around turns; and (2):
    a. Make sure that the brakes are properly balanced.
    b. Keep the cargo as close to the ground as possible.
    c. Keep the fifth wheel free play as small as possible.

29. Why should you be sure that the fifth wheel plate is greased as required?
    a. To ensure a good electrical connection.
    b. To prevent steering problems.
    c. To reduce heat and noise.

30. Your emergency air line breaks or gets pulled apart while you are driving. The loss of pressure will cause the:
    a. Air compressor to unload instead of pumping air.
    b. Tractor's air to dump into the trailer tank through the service line.
    c. Emergency trailer brakes to come on.

31. When connecting the glad hands press the two seals with the coupler together at what degree to each other?
    a. 45 degree.
    b. 90 degree.
    c. 180 degree.

32. Which of these statements is true?
    a. The brakes and suspension systems of combination vehicles work best with a light load.
    b. Light vehicles need more braking power to stop than heavy ones.
    c. Bobtail tractors can take longer to stop than a combination vehicle loaded to maximum gross weight.

33. Why should you lock the tractor glad hands to each other (or dummy couplers) when you are not towing a trailer?
    a. The connected brake circuit becomes a back up air tank.
    b. It will keep dirt or water out of the lines.
    c. If you didn't, you could never build system pressure.

34. When backing a tractor under a trailer you should:
    a. Always use the lowest reverse gear.
    b. Always approach the trailer at a slight angle.
    c. Do it quickly to ensure that the kingpin is locked into the fifth wheel.

35. After the trailer has been coupled to the tractor. The tractor protection control valve should be place in what position?
    a. Down.
    b. Up.
    c. Normal.

36. the fifth wheel locking lever is not locked after the jaws close around the kingpin. This means that:
    a. The trailer will not swivel on the fifth wheel.
    b. The parking lock is off and you may drive away.
    c. The coupling is not right and should be fixes before driving the coupled unit.

37. Off-tracking of cheating causes of which of these to follow the wider pass while make a turn?
    a. Tractor towing a 45-feet trailer.
    b. Tractor with two 27-feet trailer
    c. 53-feet bobtail.

38. The iron trailer supports are up and the trailer is resting on the tractor. Make sure:
    a. There is enough clearance between the upper and lower fifth wheels.
    b. The safety latch is in unlocked position.
    c. There is enough clearance between the tractor frame and the landing gear.

39. When you are uncoupling a loaded trailer you should lower the landing gear until it.
    a. Make firm contact with the ground, then crackle hits a low gear a few extra turns.
    b. Make contact with the ground and leave the trailer off the fifth wheel.
    c. Reaches the ground.

40. What will happen if the air lines are crossed when you hook up to an old trailer?
    a. The hand valve will apply the tractor brakes instead of trailer brakes.
    b. If the trailer has no spring brakes, you could drive away but you wouldn't have trailer brakes.
    c. The brakes light will come on when the brake pedal is pressed.

41. There are two things that a driver can do to prevent a rollover. They are: (1) keep the cargo as close to the ground as possible; and (2):
    a. Make sure that the brakes are properly adjusted.
    b. Keep both hands firmly on the steering wheel.
    c. Go slow around turns.

42. To stop a trailer skid you should:
    a. Use the trailer hand brakes.
    b. Release the service brakes.
    c. Countersteer.

43. If you cannot make a turn without entering another traffic lane
    a. you should turn wide when you start the turn.
    b. You should turn wide as you complete the turn.
    c. Not to make a turn. Go to another place where you won't have to cross into another lane.

44. The air line on a combination vehicle are often colored to prevent from mixing up. The emergency line is _____ the service line is _____.
   a. **Red, blue.**
   b. Black, yellow.
   c. Blue, red.

45. The semitrailer made before 1975 that are equipped with the air brakes:
   a. Usually need a glad hand converter.
   b. **Often do not have spring brakes.**
   c. Have only a service air line.

46. The air leakage rate for a combination vehicle (engine off, brakes on) should be less than _____ psi per minute.
   a. 2.
   b. 3.
   c. **4.**

47. Compare to a straight truck or bus there are _____ things to inspect in combination vehicle.
   a. Fewer.
   b. The same number.
   c. **More.**

48. When checking the trailer emergency brakes the tractor protection valve should be placed in what position?
   a. Normal.
   b. **Emergency.**
   c. Neutral.

49. In normal driving some drivers use the hand valve before the brake pedal to prevent a jackknife. Which of the statements is true?
   a. **It should not be done.**
   b. It results in less skidding than using the brake pedal alone.
   c. It is the best way to brake and keep the truck in a straight line.

50. While checking if the trailer is securely coupled to the trailer the landing gears should be.
   a. Fully raised.
   b. **Slightly raised.**
   c. Fully lowered.

51. Air and electrical lines from the tractor to the trailer should be:
   a. Fully tight but away a little looped.
   b. **Secured but with enough loop to turn.**
   c. Resting on the frame of the tractor.

52. You have a major leak in the service line and you put on the brakes. Service will escape and cause the:
   a. **Trailer emergency brakes to come on.**
   b. Trailer tank pressure to be lost.
   c. Tractor spring brakes to lock up.

53. A tractor with _____ a trailers requires the shortest amount of stopping distance.
   a. Empty.
   b. Light loaded.
   c. **Fully loaded.**

54. When you get ready to back under a semitrailer you should line up.
   a. The kingpin to engage the driver's side locking jaw first.
   b. **Directly front of the trailer.**
   c. The left rear outer dual wheel with the kingpin.

55. Off-tracking or cheating causes of which of these to follow the wider pass while making a turn?
   a. Tractor towing a 45 feet trailers.
   b. Tractor with two 27-feet trailers.
   c. 53-feet bobtail.

56. You should not back a tractor under a trailer until the whole air system is:
   a. Empty.
   b. At normal pressure.
   c. Between 60 and 80 psi.

57. After you lock the kingpin into the fifth wheel, you should check the connection by:
   a. Pulling forward 50 feet, turning right and then left.
   b. Backing up with the trailer brakes released.
   c. Pulling the tractor ahead gently with the trailer brakes locked.

58. When should you use the hand valve to park a combination vehicle?
   a. To park at loading docks.
   b. To park on a grade.
   c. Never.

59. you have coupled with a semitrailer Where should you put the iron trailer supports before driving away?
   a. Raised 1/2 way with the crank handle secured in its bracket.
   b. Fully raised with the crank handle secured in its bracket.
   c. 3 turn off the top with the crank handle secure in its bracket.

60. The safety catch for the fifth wheel locking level must be…… for a coupling to be complete.
   a. Over the locking level.
   b. Under the locking level.
   c. Straight up.

61. After you supply air to the trailer, make sure the air lines are not crossed and the trailer brakes are working. This is done by:
   a. Lifting the brake pedal.
   b. Watching your mirrors to see if the trailer lights come on.
   c. Applying and releasing the trailer- brakes and listening for the sound of the brake.

62. Before you back under a trailer, make sure that:
   a. The trailer brakes are locked.
   b. The tractor protection valve is normal.
   c. The air supply knob is in.

63. How should you test the tractor-semitrailer connection for security?
   a. Look at it carefully.
   b. Rock the trailer back and forth with the trailer brakes locked.
   c. Pull gently forward in low gear against the locked trailer brakes then look at it carefully.

64. The front trailer supports are up and the trailer is resting on the tractor. Make sure:
   a. There is enough clearance between the top of the tractor tires and nose of the trailer.
   b. There is enough clearance between the tractor frame and the landing gear.
   c. Both a and b are correct.

65. To unlock the fifth wheel the locking level should be placed in the position.
   a. Neutral.
   b. Close.
   c. Open.

66. The tractor protection valve close and the trailer emergency brakes will come on when there is a major leak in the _____ brake line.
   a. Service.
   b. Parking.
   c. Emergency.

67. When coupling, the proper position of the fifth wheel is.
   a. Level of the ground.
   b. Tilted down toward the end of the trailer.
   c. Tilted up toward the end the trailer.

68. What gear should the tractor engine be in after you uncouple the trailer and are inspecting the trailer supports?
   a. Neutral.
   b. Low reverse.
   c. High reverse.

69. When uncoupling the trailer, after you shut off the trailer air supply and lock the trailer brakes, you should:
   a. Back up gently to ease pressure on the fifth wheel.
   b. Put on your tractor parking brakes.
   c. Lower trailer landing gear.

70. You are driving a combination vehicle when the trailer breaks away, pulling apart both air lines. You expect the brakes to come on and:
   a. The trailer supply valve to stay open.
   b. The tractor to lose air pressure.
   c. The tractor protection valve to close.

Jeff Mills

The CDL Exam Book

Starry Night Publishing

Everyone has a story...

Don't spend your life trying to get published! Don't tolerate rejection! Don't do all the work and allow the publishing companies reap the rewards!

Millions of independent authors like you, are making money, publishing their stories now. Our technological know-how will take the headaches out of getting published. Let Starry Night Publishing take care of the hard parts, so you can focus on writing. You simply send us your Word Document and we do the rest. It really is that simple!

The big companies want to publish only "celebrity authors," not the average book-writer. It's almost impossible for first-time authors to get published today. This has led many authors to go the self-publishing route. Until recently, this was considered "vanity-publishing." You spent large sums of your money, to get twenty copies of your book, to give to relatives at Christmas, just so you could see your name on the cover. Now, however, the self-publishing industry allows authors to get published in a timely fashion, retain the rights to your work, keeping up to ninety-percent of your royalties, instead of the traditional five-percent.

We've opened up the gates, allowing you inside the world of publishing. While others charge you as much as fifteen-thousand dollars for a publishing package, we charge less than five-hundred dollars to cover copyright, ISBN, and distribution costs. Do you really want to spend all your time formatting, converting, designing a cover, and then promoting your book, because no one else will?

Our editors are professionals, able to create a top-notch book that you will be proud of. Becoming a published author is supposed to be fun, not a hassle.

At Starry Night Publishing, you submit your work, we create a professional-looking cover, a table of contents, compile your text and images into the appropriate format, convert your files for eReaders, take care of copyright information, assign an ISBN, allow you to keep one-hundred-percent of your rights, distribute your story worldwide on Amazon, Barnes & Noble and many other retailers, and write you a check for your royalties. There are no other hidden fees involved! You don't pay extra for a cover, or to keep your book in print. We promise! Everything is included! You even get a free copy of your book and unlimited half-price copies.

In nine short years, we've published more than four thousand books, compared to the major publishing houses which only add an average of six new titles per year. We will publish your fiction, or non-fiction books about anything, and look forward to reading your stories and sharing them with the world.

We sincerely hope that you will join the growing Starry Night Publishing family, become a published author, and gain the world-wide exposure that you deserve. You deserve to succeed. Success comes to those who make opportunities happen, not those who wait for opportunities to happen. You just have to try. Thanks for joining us on our journey.

www.starrynightpublishing.com

www.facebook.com/starrynightpublishing/

Made in the USA
Middletown, DE
19 February 2025